To Mary and Richard

Enjoy!

Jan and J. Nelson

1994

...and the
Kansas Wind
Blows

...and the
Kansas Wind
Blows

Raymond S. Nelson

Art work by
R. Stanley Nelson

Hearth
Hearth Publishing
A Division of Multi Business Press
Hillsboro, Kansas

. . . and the Kansas Wind Blows

First Edition
Printed in the United States of America
    1st Printing — 1991
    2nd Printing — 1992
    3rd Printing — 1993

Cover Photography by Mike Blair
Printed by Multi Business Press, Hillsboro, KS

Library of Congress Catalog Number: 91-70831

ISBN 0-9627947-1-6

Writing Poetry

How does a person write poetry? As you might expect, poets disagree. But most agree that poetry communicates in a roundabout way through images of sight, sound, smell, taste, and touch. Therefore the poet tries to select images or scenes that will convey the idea or feeling he has in mind. The poet thus says, "My love is a red, red rose" rather than saying "My love is an attractive, pretty woman." The first is poetry; the second is prose. The first generates all kinds of pleasant associations; the second is flat and unimaginative.

How then do I write poetry? It depends on the kind of poetry I wish to write. I write lyric poetry and narrative poetry.

If I wish to write a narrative poem about Jesse Chisholm, say, I read extensively about the man and his time. I learn all I can about his character and his accomplishments. Then after I have read widely, I jot down the major ideas that occur to me — the most important things. What key idea do I wish to convey, I ask myself. Then I begin to write the poem. At this stage I do not yet know what form the poem will take. I do not yet know whether I will rhyme it or not. I do not yet know whether I wish to use a four foot line or a five foot line, or whether I wish to use a metric line at all. I simply begin.

Sometimes the process works the first try. More commonly, however, I experience several false starts. But I write. And I throw away the pages of false beginnings.

I prefer metric poetry to free verse, but I try all forms to see what fits the subject matter best. And, strangely, once I get started with a congenial line and rhythm (I must omit technical terms here like iambic or anapestic feet as well as tetrameter and pentameter line lengths). The narrative line carries the poem. If I decide to rhyme the poem, the writing process leads me to the form I ultimately choose. I choose everyday words as much as I can, and simple words. Then I use a rhyming dictionary to remind me of words I already know, words that will fit the place and the sense. Sometimes the rhyme leads to an idea, and I incorporate that. And, always, I select words that generate images in the course of telling the story.

After I have written the poem, I leave it for a day or two. When I come back to the draft, I see errors and gaps that I did not notice in the heat of composition. In revision, however, I change words (seeking always the most concrete, specific term or image), relocate stanzas or lines, and fill in gaps. I have my wife read every poem and make suggestions. Whatever does not satisfy her, I rework. After several days and sometimes weeks, the text is pretty well fixed and I add the poem to my collection.

Lyric poems are similar to narrative poems in many ways, but feeling is the central concern rather than a story line. The lyric poet seeks to convey an emotion of love or friendship or warmth or coldness or pleasure. The poet already knows what he needs to know, and knows what he feels. He needs then to decide on form and approach (just like the narrative poet).

Again, I simply begin to write and see what comes out.

I experience false starts. But after I write for awhile, the emotion becomes associated with ideas and images to the extent that the poem takes shape. There is a sense in which the poem writes itself — but not without thought and effort. Line length, rhyme or unrhyme, stanza length, completeness are a few of the elements that need to be considered in the very process of writing. Some poems emerge fairly complete and finished. Most require revision and reworking several times, though the basic structure stays the same.

There remain the questions of word choice and grammatical structure. I have chosen to use common words whenever possible. I use exact words as much as I can, even technical words if necessary. But I want my poems to be understood by most readers, and I use ordinary language as a consequence. I enjoy using single syllable words; I avoid long complicated words as a rule. I also prefer regular English syntax to cryptic, strange constructions. As much as possible I use standard word order and common constructions.

I try to use punctuation that cues the reader to pause at places other than the end of lines. Some lines are run-on, and many pause within the lines. Such varied constructions add other interests to the poetry. Thus, the sounds of the poetry reinforce the meaning, and the total impression becomes a source of pleasure. For poetry is best when read aloud by an effective reader.

Poetry fuses the poet's thought and feeling with sound. It compresses experience into a small space so that the reader or listener can absorb the message easily. Poetry does in a few lines or pages what it takes dozens of prose pages to accomplish. Thus poetry is characteristically compressed, and it is indirect or roundabout in its strategy, a point I made earlier.

In all of this I try to create an art-form that engages the reader's response. I try to engage the reader's thought and feeling as he or she responds to the range of images and sounds offered. I want the reader to experience pleasure in the process of imagining the scenes presented and the senses addressed. If the poem works, the reader may think, "That's exactly right. That's what I thought." And if that happens, I feel good.

The poems which follow illustrate the process. You are invited to enjoy them and to profit from them. Use them in classes or programs or speeches or papers. Then write some yourself, using my suggestions on how to write. Poetry is the oldest form of writing, and still one of the finest.

List of Poems

The Land

The People

List of Illustrations

To Margaret

T H E   L A N D

HAIKU

The restless wind blows
From the south to tip the trees
In constant homage.

. . . AND THE KANSAS WIND BLOWS

It sings a ceaseless melody
Across the Great High Plains.
It rustles through the cottonwoods
And whispers in the wheat;
The heron's feathers flutter
As waves splash on the beach.
It moans in shuttered windows
And makes the wind-chimes ring;
The flags stand at attention
Or snap in sharp salutes.
The breezes pause at sunrise
But sound tattoo by noon,
Crescendo into evening,
Complain the whole night through.
Summer zephyrs, wintry gales
Provide rich harmonies
As Nature breathes in minor chords
And sings incessantly.

KANSAS PLANTS

There are dozens of plants native to Kansas as any good botanical book makes clear. I have written about only a few of them.

The yucca thrives in the arid parts of western Kansas and eastern Colorado. It multiplies like rabbits through the seeds that scatter far and wide — seeds, by the way, that come from blossoms pollinated by the yucca moth. The yucca moth lays its eggs so that the larvae feed on some of the seeds in the seed pod. When the seeds are ripe, the pods break open and the wind and birds distribute whatever seeds are left. The plant needs the moth and the moth needs the plant. It's a nice arrangement. Yucca has many nicknames, several of which are in the poem: silkgrass, beargrass, curly-hair, soapweed (Indians used the root for a kind of soap), Spanish bayonet, Adam's needle, and God's candle.

The cactus does not need much water, and exists in dozens of varieties across the plains. The most noteworthy thing about cactus other than its thorns and its ability to thrive with very little rain is the colorful blossom which bursts out from time to time — reds, yellows, oranges.

The Sunflower (*Helianthus*) became the official state flower in 1903. Senator George Morehouse, sponsor of the act, wrote about the flower: "This native wild flower is common throughout our borders, and is hardy and conspicuous. It lifts its head in triumph along our most beautiful and classic valleys and mingles its cheerful light with the verdure of expanding prairies." Kansas has become known as "The Sunflower State" as the result of the legislative action.

Queen Anne's Lace is a dainty white flower that graces the meadows and pastures and valleys of eastern Kansas. It needs more moisture than yucca and cacti, and flourishes where rains fall more often. It is a remarkably delicate blossom made up of thousands of tiny white particles — tiny blossoms in their own right. It often measures four to five inches across its convex curve. It is a lowly wild carrot, in fact, but the stem rises two to three feet to a regal display of chaste beauty.

The tumbleweed is properly the Russian thistle. It is not native to Kansas, but was introduced to the plains during the nineteenth century. It grows lustily in dry places, and when mature, dries and breaks from the root. It then rolls across the prairie as the winds drive it along, filling ditches and fence rows and towns. During the worst days of the drought in the thirties, crops would not grow. But the Russian thistle did, so some farmers mowed it, raked it, and made silage out of it to feed the cattle.

Clematis is also not native to the plains, but it does grow well in places where it can be watered such as in towns and cities. It is colorful and beautiful, and it tends to climb high on trellises and trees.

QUEEN ANNE'S LACE

The snowy crown of Queen Anne's Lace
Surpasses rarest human works of art,
A family crest and coat of arms
Designed in green and white, with trace
Of royal purple at its heart,
A cynosure of regal forms.

How strange that lowly figures rise
To eminence at times, that kings
Have sprung from peasant loins. How strange
That Queen Anne's Lace, the meadow's prize,
From humble root each season springs —
A carrot wild — how singularly strange.

THE SUNFLOWER

The sunflower stands
In sturdy gold and black
Across the state.
At break of dawn
It scans the heavens
For a glimpse of Helios —
The god who runs
His daily race —
And, buoyant, sways
In the light of day.
It radiates a glory
From the many blooms
That swell its crown,
Corolla of the plain.

CACTI

Prickly, thorny cactus spines
Stay barren as hot desert sands
Until they burst in glorious bloom
Of radiant color, dainty form,
To make a paradise of hell
As inner beauty breaks its shell.

TUMBLEWEEDS

The weeds roll on incessantly
As south winds press and drive,
They tumble, fumble, nervously
As if they are alive.

Some gather in great crowds at times
At fence rows (clad in browns),
Some fill the railroad ditches full
And some pile high in towns.

They play at dodge-em on the roads
With cars and trucks the odds,
They win and keep on rolling through
Or lose — and end up shards.

YUCCA

Stalwart sentinel, en garde!
Let your Spanish bayonet
Assure that meddlers stand at bay
Far from Silkgrass, Beargrass,
Curly-hair, and Soapweed.
Stand in sturdy pride of place
On open western range,
Clad in martial green and white,
Hues that speak in silence
Of great strength and age.
Should a worthy, ragged
Pilgrim pause to mend a cloak,
Let him use old Adam's Needle
With its gray-green thread
To suture up the seams.

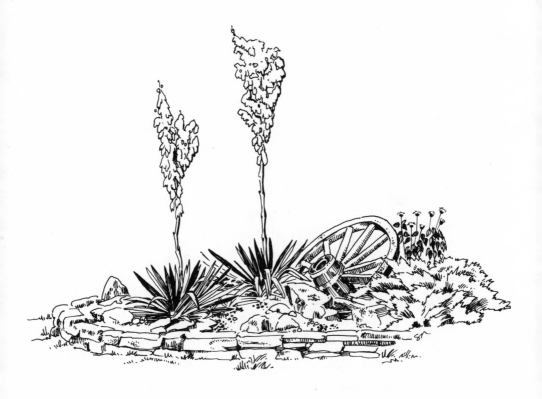

CLEMATIS

Clematis and a sweetgum tree
Grow neighbors in our yard;
An arbor serves the lusty vine,
The sentinel stands guard.

The vine runs rampant on the frame,
Its arms reach every way,
The tree stands silently nearby,
Enticingly each day.

The tendrils of the vine reach out,
They stretch and grasp and grope,
The arbor is too small and low,
The leaders want more scope.

The waving tendrils fasten high
In branches of the tree,
They wrap themselves around the twigs
Secure as they can be.

The tree supports the vine, tis true,
The vine loves sweetgum strength,
The pair survive in amity
And dally at great length.

A Venus and a Mars they seem,
Soft dalliance and brawn,
The goddess clinging to her love,
The god erect full drawn.

A marriage of a sort it is,
A common-law affair;
The two embrace and blend at will
As summer's life they share.

Memo to: The Lord

Date: February, 1981
Re: Kansas Weather

Have you noticed, Lord?
I hate to mention it again,
But we need rain.
The ground is baked and dry —
Even cracked in parts —
And each day brings a cloudless sky.

And while I'm at it, Lord,
It's unseasonably warm.
It's not yet March,
But all the buds are great
And I'm afraid a sudden frost
Will blight the life at springtime's gate.

I'm just your servant, Lord,
And you're in charge, of course.
I only wondered
If you'd heard our point of view?
But now I've had my say
So, Lord, I'll leave our cares to you.

EARLY EXPLORERS

Lewis and Clark opened exploration of the newly purchased Louisiana Territory from 1803-1806. They traveled up the Missouri River, across the Rockies, all the way to the Pacific Ocean. In 1806-1807, Zebulon Pike explored what became Kansas Territory, beginning at the Missouri River. He followed the Arkansas River to its source and, in the process, discovered the mountain peak in Colorado which bears his name. These explorers made careful notes and maps about the country they saw. Their skill and accuracy are amazing.

Stephen Long, accompanied by a botanist, zoologist, geologist, painter and other technical experts, began a westward journey from Pittsburgh in the east to the Rockies in the west. He details Kansas Territory with excellent care along with other sections of the country. He and his men made extensive study of the land, with its trees, plants, animals, and topography; Indian customs and tribes; daily experiences, including weather and location (by longitude and latitude).

Journal entries, maps, letters, notes on Indian life and language, financial records, and other such materials exist yet today, many of them published. They tell of hardships and bad experiences as well as successes and pleasures. Long writes about the terrain which is now Colorado and much of Kansas. "In regard to this extensive section of country, we do not hesitate in giving the opinion, that it is almost wholly unfit for cultivation. . . . The scarcity of wood and water, almost uniformly prevalent, will prove an insuperable obstacle in the way of settling the country. . . . This region, however, viewed as a frontier, may prove of infinite importance to the United States, inasmuch as it is calculated to serve as a barrier to prevent too great an extension of our population westward, and secure us against the machinations or incursions of an enemy. . . ."

THE GREAT AMERICAN DESERT

When Pike and Long explored the land
They traversed far and wide,
They mapped the rivers and the plains
And made long lists beside

Of birds and animals and plants,
Of insects, rocks, and trees.
They measured north and south with care
And registered degrees.

The Rockies were their western bound
Big Muddy to the east,
The Platte the northern edge, the Red
Where southern ventures ceased.

They thought these treeless miles were waste —
A buffer to the west —
They said no farm or ranch could thrive;
Best leave these lands at rest.

Colorado to the west was lean
And arid in the main,
With yucca, cactus, dusty sage
In canyons and the plain.

Kansas and Nebraska shared
A semi-arid state
Where western regions dry and sere
Held forth a doubtful fate.

Yet settlers came and ploughed the ground —
Some made it, others left.
Some planted hardy rugged crops
While neighbors were bereft.

Irrigation came in time —
More farmers could survive.
The oil and feedlots added depth
And Kansas stayed alive.

Old Pike and Long were largely right —
Drouths come most years. Not much
Has changed. At risk are beasts and crops —
There *is* a desert touch.

SUNSET

Apollo paints the western sky
Each evening with most brilliant hues,
His palette filled with reds and blues
And orange, brushing wide and high.

The scenes are never quite the same:
Infinity the source, pure art
The means, the Titan does his part
Routinely, artist of great fame.

THE FLINT HILLS

The sunrise gilds the wintry hills
In all their quiet eminence,
Ancient mountains, hoar and worn
By frost and wind and rain and time.
Long bluegrass stems and fronds hang bent
Beneath their loads of ice and snow.
The snowclad grasses glisten gold
And silver as lean cattle stir
And winter birds seek seeds and grain
In lowlands and secluded glens.
But flowing time brings thaws, then spring,
With April rains and blooms of May
That robe the undulating hills
With fabric richer than a lord's.
The radiant light of dawn refracts
In drops of dew that drape each stem
And web with diamond necklaces.
The hills become a wonderland
Of color and expanse, where views
To north, to east, to south, or west
Are unobstructed. Trees hug close
To valley streams — some cottonwood
Some elm, some cedar. Meadowlarks
Abound to sing their joyous song,
And insects drone throughout the day.

A month or two, and morning rays
Shine on a variegated quilt
Of russets, tans, and browns, so wrought
By scorching heat and lingering drouth,
The scene transformed. The limestone scarps
Accent the view with whites and grays,
And flinty shards defy all plows
To shear the sod. Yet cattle, deer,
Shy rodents, reptiles, birds and bees
Continue on their rounds at dawn
And dusk, surviving cannily
Against great odds. The grand old hills
Are never quite the same from day
To day, yet every day inspires
A sense of wonder and of awe.

COTTONWOOD

The cottonwood survives. It stands
In stately splendor on a plain
Or thicket in alluvial sands.

Its wondrous mantle seems a fane,
A spreading canopy of green
Despite hot sun and little rain.

Its massive bole commands the scene
With deep-ridged bark and lofty limb,
Though often scarred through nature's spleen.

When stresses mount, and times are grim,
The cottonwood survives to grace
The Great High Plains with sturdy vim —

Not much for lumber, make the case,
The cottonwood fulfills its place
In wooded vales or open space.

The Cottonwood became the official
state tree in 1937.

VERY LIKE A FACE

I watch the changing image
  On the wide screen of the sky
As ever-drifting puffballs
  Converge, disperse, on high.

Some clouds reach to the zenith
  From edges far below,
Or stretch from east to western
  Rim in stunning show.

They soar aloft or hover,
  They linger or they race,
They beautify the landscape
  And lighten heaven's face.

Sometimes they look like puppies —
  Or very like a face —
Or trees — or range of mountains —
  Or dainty, frilly lace.

I like to lie on greensward
  And idly watch the screen
Kaleidoscopically
  Turn and shift the scene.

Most clouds are white and fluffy,
  Set sharp against bright blue,
Unless approaching sunset
  Creates a rosy hue.

Some are like a canopy —
  They hide the sun from sight —
As if drawn blinds at noontime
  Had changed the day to night.

A few are dark and eerie.
  They threaten life and limb
When lightning bolts or funnels
  Descend from deep within.

Each Kansas vista varies,
  Delighting watchful eye —
The sky is always different
  As clouds scud low or high.

THE BUFFALO

I

Young Eagle sat astride his mount
To view the herd he could not count,
A mass of bison moving slow
In ordered files. They seemed to flow
In rhythmic waves across the plain
In groups that came and came and came,
Great-shouldered bulls with careful eye
On stately harems coursing by
In shoals, a living sea that dyed
The bluestem black. The warrior eyed
The dusty scene, the source of hide
And food, yet made no move to ride
Or shoot, lest he stampede the herd.
Young Eagle soon must bring the word
To tribesmen that the beasts had come,
The cows and calves had safely swum
The Cimarron and now arrived
On summer grounds. They had survived
The migrant miles, a stirring sight —
Magnificent in grace and might.

THE BUFFALO

II

The Kanzas left their chores when word
Of bison came. Excitement stirred
The camp as men and women ran
For gear they knew they'd need. Each clan
Was eager for the hunt. The men
Chose arrows, bows, and ponies, then
Followed by the women, found
The herd. They slowly spread around
The beasts, choosing each a cow
Or calf as prize. Then at a "Now"
They charged the grazing buffalo,
Who surged into a churning flow
Of living water on the plain.
Each brave raced too, his single aim
The noble animal he chose
Before the race. At hour's close
The tribe had killed enough to feed
All handsomely and serve a need
Or two beside. The herd soon trod
And grazed in quiet on the sod.

BUFFALO

III

The shaggy bison filled the plain
Till white men, part to entertain,
Part to harvest pelts and meat,
And part to clear the range for wheat,
Combined to practice genocide.
They slaughtered buffalo, they plied
A trade in skins, but left the rest
As carrion to rot. The West
Was built on buffalo, but men
Like Cody and Bill Mathewson
Left skulls and skeletons in piles
That settlers gathered up for miles
And sold to factors in the East.
The disappearance of the beast
From prairies wild and vast and lone,
Reduced to chips and horn and bone
From vanished grandeur, grace, and strength,
Suggests all earthly gain at length
Involves great loss. Magnificence
Is sometimes sold for paltry pence.

> The Buffalo became the State Animal
> in 1955.

26

CONSIDER THE TURTLE

The turtle lives in a bony box —
An improbable creature, truth to say.
It thinks long thoughts as it slowly moves
Through the prairie grasses on its way
To its cronies or larder far or near
In mild-mannered purpose night or day.

Passive resistance is ever its ploy —
It closes up tight when faced with fray.
It's revered round the world, even sacred to some;
In myth it supports this earth of clay.
Inscrutable creature, head held high,
Triassic survivor, still here today.

The box turtle became the
state reptile in 1986.

THE CARDINAL

Pretty, Pretty, Pretty,
    Pretty, Pretty, Pretty.
Those liquid notes mean "keep in touch,"
One redbird to another,
A prelude to the flaming red
That flashes soon from cover.

Pretty, Pretty, Pretty,
    Pretty, Pretty, Pretty.
The redbird brightens winter's drab.
He contrasts with the snow
And stays as well for summer's green —
A grace on any bough.

THE HAWK

He keeps a lonely vigil
On a fence post or a pole
Surveying fields and ditches
For rabbits or a vole.

He preens himself at leisure —
Each feather in its place —
While watching from his vantage
The miles of open space.

He lords it on the prairie,
He soars in sovereign ease,
He stoops with ruthless talon
Unwary life to seize.

Skilled raptor of the heartland,
He lives by nature's laws,
No evil in his actions
Though life from death he draws.

FIRST SNOW

The ground this morning was all white,
The trees festooned with snow. The roads
Were clogged, the bushes bowed, and drifts,
Like dunes, stretched smoothly out of sight.

My steps were muffled, sounds subdued,
The scene all new and strange as I
With animals and birds approached
A world we had till then not viewed.

A trace of smoke hung in the air,
But otherwise the air was crisp
And clear, filtered by the flakes
That lay profusely everywhere.

The sun's rays glistened on the ice
And crystals, set like solitaires,
As heaven and waiting earth joined hands
In a newly fashioned paradise.

A falcon soared on high in search
Of prey, a crow flapped lazily
Afar, and seven sparrows watched
The feeder from an arbor perch.

I lived my idyll until noon
When sounds of steel on stone announced
The plow had come and I must leave
For town and daily round resume.

BEEHIVE

A queen with her ladies in waiting
Rules firmly in feudal accord,
Accepts protocol from her minions
And homage from every last lord.

Her queendom is ancient and stable,
Relationships settled and sure.
She rules with an iron precision,
Enjoys a rich reign quite secure.

The ladies in waiting are faithful
They spend themselves to the last dime,
They dance in their utter devotion,
They offer their bounty sublime.

The gentlemen serve on short notice —
They give of their all to the cause,
They render full strength to their sovereign
Observing her system of laws.

No patriarch ever was better;
She rules her dominion with grace.
Her monarchy functions superbly
With every last lackey in place.

WINTER WHEAT

The heavy heads of amber wheat
That wave on Kansas plains in June
Invite a hungry world to eat,

To share in bread and pasta, boon
That early settlers brought as seed,
Hard Turkey Red most opportune.

That winter wheat, a hardy breed,
Transformed the early farmer's way
And led to yields that millions feed.

For golden wheat we share today
We bow to God — and men — to say
"Our thanks for all that fills this tray."

THE PEOPLE

KANSAS WINDS

They twirl and swirl the skirts of Spring
In form as graceful as a lass
Beguiling time in a Highland Fling.

THE KEEPER OF THE PLAINS

He stands in solitary grandeur
Where two rivers meet,
Hands high in supplication
To the Great Spirit
Who makes all one.

He stands in supple grace
While winds speak softly through
His feathered headdress,
Resilient and brave,
To say that everything is holy.

He stands in strength,
His back a supple bow,
Withstanding stress and strain —
His piercing eyes fixed firmly
On a future where all peoples
Live in peace and plenty.

> Blackbear Bosin's *Keeper*
> stands at the confluence
> of the Arkansas and Little
> Arkansas Rivers in Wichita.

37

KANSAS

The Kanza People of the Wind
Wrung their living from the land
Till storied herds of bison thinned
From the white man's gun and ruthless hand.

They lived in simple dignity
With brother Pawnee and Osage
Till settlers in cupidity
Surveyed the land and set the stage

For carnage virulent and red
As Kanzas fought to save their land
From predators who quickly spread
And threatened to devour the band.

Chief White Plume met with men of state
Negotiating lands and life,
But broken treaties, soon and late,
Provoked long years of bloody strife.

The Southwind People left the Kaw
To settlers in their turn, but left
A heritage of pride. They saw
Their name enshrined (themselves bereft).

> *Kanza* (or *Kaw*) means "The Wind
> People," among other speculations.

CORONADO

I remember it as yesterday.
We had followed Turk southeast until
The army came to the Great Barranca, a cut
That deeply scarred the earth, and Don Vasquez
At last decided that Isopete
Was right — that rascal Turk had led us far
Astray. What then to do? Already June,
There was no time to lose. The general chose
Full thirty men to travel north with him
And left the rest to make their way back west
Despite great disappointment. So we went.

I, Juan Jaramillo, served a man
Most brave yet gentle, severed scion of
His sire's estate, late come to Mexico
To seek his fortune, named Francisco
Vasquez de Coronado. Fortune smiled.
Francisco wed Beatriz, wealthy dame,
And soon was chosen leader of a band
To search the inner reaches of New Earth.

We traveled north with Sopete our guide
And thirty valorous, hardy, hand-picked men.
We crossed the Arkansas at Ford. We hoped
To find Quivira still, you see. We'd been
In quest of Seven Golden Cities then
A year or more, and we were worn and gaunt.
But Coronado, gracious lord, was sure

We'd find them now. We met some Indians camped
Nearby, Quiviras sure, and learned our goal
Was near at hand. Our leader sat him down
To write Tatarrax, giant man and chief
Of the Wichitas. The letter sent,
The Don led out past Pawnee Rock, and soon
To Great Bend on the River of Quivira,
Cow Creek, Long Branch, even Jarvis Creek.
We camped in hopes of El Dorado wealth.

The Turk was captive in a tent, well out
Of sight, but troublesome because he still
Connived to do us harm. Our gentle lord
At long last gave command to silence him
Forever. Tabas was the place, a tent
The scene, garroting him the means they chose.
They buried him in secrecy that night.

We spent a month enjoying maize and beans,
Buffalo and fish, observing life
In round grass huts, while resting on the plain.
We found no gold, no precious gems, no prize
Such as we sought. The land itself was good,
The rivers fine. But time was racing, fall
Quite near, provisions low, and clothing light.

We left in August, fifteen forty-one,
To join the army at Tigeux and found
Them there. In all we spent two years, and more,
In fruitless search for gold. We failed in that
But gained great glory as the first to map
New Spain in service of our glorious king,
Charles the Fifth of Spain, Imperial Lord.

MADONNA OF THE TRAIL

She strides with cleareyed purpose
On the well trod western trail,
Her chin is firm as granite,
Her figure strong and hale.

She wears a simple bonnet,
A modest cloak and dress,
All symbols of her spirit
Of quiet sturdiness.

She bears a babe, a nursling,
And leads a clinging lad,
The others follow stairstep
With the ox-team and their dad.

She shares her husband's vision
Of life on fruitful land,
She steps into the future,
The present well in hand.

The Madonna of the Trail statue by August Leimbach
of St. Louis stands in Council Grove.

JESSE CHISHOLM

He was my friend. He never let a man
Go cold or hungry from his door. I can
Vouch for that. He never wore a gun.
They welcomed him in Indian camps as one
Of them as freely as the whites who threw
Their lot with him. He hurt no man. He knew
The Indian tongues, the white man's too, and told
The truth. When treaties failed, when drumbeats rolled,
He went between to mark the way to peace.
He plied his skills with both. He sought release
Of captives — children that he ransomed, sent
On home or added to his flock. He went
Just where he pleased, a friend to all. He took
A wife and had two sons, but closed that book
When death took her — Elizabeth. In time
He married Sa Kar Kar, as yet in prime
Of life, and had four children more. He made
More Posts, he prospered well, his stock in trade
The things the army and the Indians sought.
He knew the trails like no one else and taught
Them handily. Half Scotch, half Cherokee
Himself, he loved the hills and wide prairie.
We rode together many times, and I
Still hear his voice. He said one day, "I try
To live in peace with men. All folks are kin
To me. The Great Spirit works from deep within
To lead us all to peace." His name lives on,
The Chisholm Trail mute witness to a life
Committed to men living without strife.

As spoken by W. R. Mead, early developer in Wichita.

ABILENE

Smoky Hill

Arkansas

NEWTON

Ninnescah

WICHITA

Chikaski

WELLINGTON

CALDWELL

Salt Fork — MEDFORD

POND CREEK

Canadian

ENID

DOVER

Cimarron

KINGFISHER

Jesse
Chisholm's
Grave

GEARY

OKLAHOMA CITY

EL RENO

YUKON

So. Canadian

CHICKASHA

DUNCAN

OKLA.

ADDINGTON

TEXAS

WAURIKA

RYAN

RED RIVER
STATION

Red River

BOWIE

DECATUR

FORT WORTH

DALLAS

Colorado

HILLSBORO

WACO

TEMPLE

Trinity

AUSTIN

SAN MARCOS

NEW BRAUNFELS

GONZALES

SAN ANTONIO

CUERO

Rio Grande

LAREDO

CORPUS CHRISTI

Gulf of Mexico

The Chisholm Trail

PIONEER WOMAN I

A time we had of it. We camped
In tents till sod was turned and sowed.
First things first. Then we cut
A dugout in a limestone ridge.
The rock was soft, the walls stood firm,
The floor was dirt, the roof of logs
Covered up with branches and
A layer of sod. We lived with rain
And snakes and mice, with dust and dirt,
Till we built a clapboard house
And felt like lords. But hail and drouth
Caused crops to fail, and sickness took
My only child — no doctor near at hand.
I was alone — all, all alone —
For days on end as Matt toiled on.
I read each book a dozen times,
I quilted at my frame. I walked
For miles to see my neighbor friends,
But that was rare. I doubted God,
I near went mad with loneliness
And hardship. Other times were good,
Of course, and as the years flowed by
We had another son. And Matt
Had time for home and me as well
As field work. Crops were good some years
And bad in others. But we held
Our course, and now in age I hold
With those who say that life is in
The living, come what may each day.

A bronze statue, "Three Women Walking" (1981) by Francisco Zuniga, stands on The Wichita State University Campus.

PIONEER WOMAN II

She left her home in Gotham Square,
Her husband having written all was set.
He'd built a sod house on the claim
And now he needed her out there.

She took a train, she rode four days,
She crossed the river on a barge,
She traveled in a crowded coach
Sustained by dreams despite delays.

She pressed ahead the last few miles
With a simple wagon box and team,
Arriving at the homestead late,
Exhausted, punchy, yet all smiles.

The soddie was a dugout, part
Below the turf, and part above,
Plastered walls and earthen floor,
With table, chairs, and bed to start.

She daily filled her part with grace,
Slaving in the house or field,
Planting, hoeing, cooking, glad
To share the challenge of the place.

She carried water, fed the sow,
Stored potatoes, apples, flour,
Pumpkins, melons, dried some meat
And salted more, then milked the cow.

She made her clothes from calico
Or gingham, patched his socks and shirt,
His overalls and coat, with patch
On patch, while there were shreds to sew.

She hosted neighbors in her turn
For birthday parties, holidays,
For preaching, singing, quilting bees,
Fine chance to share and talk and learn.

She rarely went to town to shop —
He did that — for roads were mires
In rain, and dust-bowls in the sun
With town a twelve-mile, all-day stop.

She shared his bed, and children came
By ones and twos, until sheer need
Cried out for space, and rooms were built,
And then in time a house to frame.

They survived through drouth and flood,
Adding acres, earning more,
Children helping, thriving well
Together through bad years and good.

Till gray and stooped, with snapping eyes,
She had it all: a spacious farm
And gracious house, a loving mate,
A growing tribe: true wealth as prize.

RELICS

The skeletons of vanished dreams
Lie scattered on the plains
As broken windmills, weathered walls
Stand idly near grown lanes.

The isolated ruins stand
Mute witness to a past
When sturdy pioneers grew roots
And built as though to last.

But droughts and storms came cycling on
And one by one dreams died,
And slowly, one by one, men left,
And left their houses wide.

Such relics of a bygone day
Speak silently of loss,
Of broken hearts and homes and lives —
As bitter as a cross.

The Pony Express statue by Richard Bergen of Salina
stands at Marysville.

THE PONY EXPRESS

You say you wonder what the trail was like.
I never will forget those days, I'll strike
A fire first, then tell a tale. I rode
With Keetley, Frye and Haslam — men I owe
A lot to. Men whose strength and courage taught
Me early not to quit, but that I ought
To finish what I start. I watched that first
Guy touch the ground at Elwood in a burst
Of fire from St. Jo. He waved and spurred
His mustang right through town, a graceful bird
In flight. I caught the fever, sensed the pride
That filled his bones. I got my chance to ride
From Marysville to Summit, near the Platte,
And rode that route one month. I'd tossed my hat
Into the ring. I loved the grueling pace
But hardly settled in my weekly race
When Utah was all in flames. Paiute braves
Had rampaged — killing, burning, thieving waves
Of angry warriors bound to take their lands
Again from white men gaining ground. My hands
Were free in Kansas, so I volunteered
To join the riders in the West. I feared
But little in those days. And got my way.
My hero — Pony Bob — and I would stray
Quite far afield to miss the enemy.
And mostly did. But once I raced with three
Young Utes and made it through, though nicked right here.

My horse was faster, stronger, tougher — near
Twice as good. But it was some close call.
One rider — just one — lost his life in all
The miles racked up, though many station men
Were killed and buried near the trail. But then
The mountains and the snows and floods were grim,
Much worse in ways than Indian wrath. To swim
A swollen flood, or fight a mountain pass
Filled deep with snow, called for a special class
Of heroes — unsung heroes — sworn to do
A job — and did it. News that made it through
Each week kept California with the North
And helped the Union cause. The twenty-fourth
Of April marks the day I joined the ranks
Of those brave souls, a breed that I give thanks
I came to know. I'm glad I'm here to praise
The men who lived the glory of those days.

MY QUILTS

Gladys, let me tell about my quilts.
They're all we had as comforters at first,
When John and I staked out this claim. That chest
Across the room could hold them all. I made
A Crazy Quilt from scraps I'd saved for months
Before we came. Scraps of every kind:
Denim, gingham, ticking, calico —
Even bits of wool. It's on the bottom, now,
Almost worn out. Then when we came out here
I made a Double Wedding Ring for best,
And Barbara, my neighbor, helped me piece
Some more — and I helped her, of course. It's all
We had for many years. And they were warm.
Heavy, but warm. My prize — here, let me show
My prize — a Friendship Quilt! The Ladies Aid
Made blocks that told of memories we share
From forty years of work. They appliqued
Or pieced the blocks, then stitched them — thirty-six —
Into this quilt to grace our bed. I use
It sparingly. I want my daughter Ann
To have it as an heirloom when I'm gone.
These quilts could tell great stories as we shared
Our joys and fears (if they could speak). We loved
And slept and talked. We laughed and cried as years
Rolled by, while quilts were all we had to keep
Us warm. We don't use them much today
But keep them to remember days gone by.

PIONEERS

Some lived in dugouts in a hill
Or sod huts on the plain until
The field produced enough to fill
The bins. Then houses came at will.

They built with local store and stock —
With prairie scrub and cottonwoods,
Or limestone slab, or quarried rock,
Though Conestogas soon brought goods

Like glass and lumber, tin and brick,
To shape homes like they'd known before.
They left their tiny huts as quick
As time and means afforded more.

They came and went the kitchen door
Those early years, and sat in chairs
At table near a stove where less and more
Were shared in candor without airs.

Their life was unpretentious, spare,
And lean, but rich in kin and friend.
They shared life's sorrow, joy, and care
In pioneer courage without end.

KANSAS COWTOWNS

When Joe McCoy chose Abilene
To build his livestock pens,
He cleared the way for longhorn herds
And Texas cattlemen.

The few log huts and fine broad plain
Were soon a brawling town
With depot, bars, hotels, and shops
To give the place renown.

The drovers came in growing bands
By eighteen sixty-nine
To send their longhorns to the East
For countrymen to dine.

But gamblers came, loose women too,
With gunmen and their kind,
So life in Abilene was wild
Till Tom Smith made them mind.

By eighteen hundred seventy-two
The farmers said "Don't Come,"
So drovers turned to Ellsworth town
And brought with them the scum.

The Kansas and Pacific line
Cut Ellsworth quite in two —
The proper folk lived to the north
Far from the southern crew.

The businessmen and bankers throve
As herds of cattle came,
But wild folk tore the town apart,
Gave Ellsworth a bad name.

Prosperity was brief — a year
Or two — and fortune changed.
The drovers came to Wichita
Where yards were all arranged.

But Newton shared the stage those years
With "Hide Park" south of town,
Where desperadoes quarreled free
And shot each other down.

The cattlemen brought wealth to town
Where gambling stakes went high,
The Gold Rooms fleeced them at such play
And hung them out to dry.

The Santa Fe made Wichita
The grandest of the grand,
The largest and the noisiest
Of cowtowns in the land.

Her stockyards were well built and large,
The herds in great supply,
So Wichita increased in wealth
As shippers came to buy.

Based on a sketch in Joseph G. McCoy's *Historic Sketches of the Cattle Trade of the West and Southwest* (1874)

It couldn't last, the bubble burst,
The herds went south and west . . .
New trails were blazed, new fords explored
As drovers tried their best.

The Texas cattle brought disease
To animals on hand
So local ranchers pushed for laws
To have the longhorns banned.

As quarantines moved west, and west,
Dodge City got the trade,
The last great center for the cows
Emerged as yards were made.

Dodge City was a wicked place
Before the cattle came.
A lawless town from early days,
It had a lusty name.

And so it stayed a ten year span
As drovers came that way —
An open town, a cowhand's sport —
With few to say them nay.

By eighteen hundred eighty-three
Dodge City had to change.
The Texans kept their herds at home
And sold them from the range.

At Caldwell on the Chisholm Trail
The cattlemen did well;
They leased lands from the Cherokees
For stock they'd buy and sell.

But blizzards came in 'eighty-six
That caused them loss and woe,
Then legal battles closed the range
And herding had to go.

Some famous names like Masterson
Or Earp, or Allison,
Or Wild Bill Hickok come to mind
As figures from the sum.

Those twenty storied years were wild,
And many tales are told,
Some true, some false, some stretched, some thin,
A mine of purest gold.

WINDWAGON THOMAS

Five cronies met in Yoakum's Bar one day
To hoist a glass and pass the time away.
It was in eighteen fifty-three, in spring,
At Westport near Missouri's northern swing.
They talked of Injuns, growing towns, and news
Back East, of Texas cattle, who to choose
For mayor in the vote to come, then heard
Commotion in the street outside. One stirred
And said he'd take a look. He found eight boys
In curious knot, their usual boistrous noise
Cut off, their eyes fixed on a strange machine.
The dogs were gone; no women could be seen.
The town seemed scared and silent, like the lull
Before a storm. The sight was strange. A hull
On wheels, white sail aloft, until a man
Pulled up before the Yoakum Bar and there began
To anchor down. He dropped the sail and set
His brakes, then disembarked and went to wet
His whistle. "Thomas is my name," he said,
"The Navigator of the Plains, I've read
Of trade with Santa Fe, and now I'm here
To make us rich as kings." The five drew near
And shared a bottle as they listened to
His plan. A fleet of ships with sails would do
The trick. Their money and his skill were all
They needed. Wind and sailing ships would haul

The gear more cheaply than expensive yoke
Of mule or ox. And faster. Soon one spoke
To say that they were not born yesterday.
They had no coin for him to throw away.
"Tell you what I'll do," this Thomas said.
"I'll sail to Council Grove, and when I've sped,
Return in nine day's time. I'll larn ye good."
The five, and many others, laughed. He could
Not cover those three hundred prairie miles
In time. They tipped their glasses up, all smiles,
And said, "We've seen the last of him, the fool."
The Navigator climbed aboard, and, cool,
Released the brake, hauled up the sail, and set
Out to the west, while swirls of dust beset
The hangers-on outside. The schooner skimmed
Across the plain as Captain Thomas trimmed
His sail and disappeared from view. The men
Went home and shared the joke with wives, and then
Forgot the matter clean. But scarce nine days
Had gone, before a voice cried out: "Friends, gaze
Into the west. Is that a sail I see?
Is that the Navigator? Can it be?"
The sail drew near the tavern door and stopped.
The wheels stood still, the lofty sheet was dropped
And Thomas said, "I thirst. Let's have a drink."
Then soon arrived the trusty five. "I think
You thought I'd fail," he said — A stratagem
To clear all minds of doubt, he offered them

A letter from the blacksmith at the Grove.
Windwagon Thomas now no longer strove
To make his point. The five that very day
Financed his plan, and huge windwagons lay
In store for Thomas and the men. No slip
Between the cup and lip must be. One ship
Was built — a mammoth bark — with twelve-foot wheels,
An eight-foot beam and twenty-five at keel,
The mast stepped well to bow. The tongue would steer
The craft, a single sail aloft. All clear,
Four men with Thomas slowly climbed aboard,
While Doctor Parker stayed ashore, but roared,
"Shove off!" The Navigator raised the sail
Then grasped the helm, prepared to catch a gale
Of wind. The monstrous schooner slowly stirred
And slowly picked up speed. The riders heard
The snapping sheet, the creaking joints, and feared
For life and limb — But soon the foursome cheered
And laughed — the wagon smoothly sailed. It cleared
Small ditches, rolled on grass, the pilot steered
It well. The mighty wagon of the wind
Would soon be bound for Santa Fe, he grinned.
The four investors looked around as far
As eye could see. The wagon seemed a star
Performer, rolling as at sea. They soon
Began to dream of fame and wealth, the boon
Of risk. The Overland to Santa Fe
Seemed quite in hand — who would say them nay?

But suddenly the tiller stuck, the craft
Began to veer. It shuddered fore and aft.
The jaunty wagon circled far and wide
As Thomas sought to turn the tide —
Almost a mile, as Thomas tried to stop.
The wagon shook, it quivered too, from top
To bottom board. One frightened man jumped clear,
His partners trembled, cowered, white with fear,
Until they also jumped the ship. The bark
Rolled on before the gale, like Noah's ark,
But Captain Thomas kept the deck. He rode
The waves of bending grass, he bravely strode
The planks — till suddenly the ship stopped short
Against a fence on Turkey Creek. The sport
Was ended, and the stint was done. No word
Would do. The five were through. They'd not be stirred
To further venture on that sea of grass.
They'd just as soon forget what came to pass.
Windwagon heard, but would not quit. He knew
He'd find some takers. Thomas was not through.
His light machine was anchored near, its sail
Awaiting wind and will to hit the trail.
He sailed away that very day as fast
As wind allowed. He set his course due west
And soon was lost to sight. He sailed away,
Say Westport folk, but might return some day.

Stanley Vestal (Walter S. Campbell)
first told this tale.

SUMMER SCENE

Weeding was the worst, we thought.
We children carried water, cut
The wood, picked apples, grapes, and pears.
We pricked our fingers as we fought
Thorn bushes for elusive fruit
To be preserved and stored downstairs

In endless rows of Mason jars
Filled with the summer's luscious wealth.
We carried trash, we fetched the mail,
We swept and dusted, did our chores
Inside and out, with playful stealth
Or boisterous noise in varied scale.

We did our share, those early years.
We labored long and hard. We filled
Our days with work, reserving play
For better times to come, when fears
Of not enough to eat were stilled.
Yet weeding was the worst, we'd say.

JOHN BROWN

Many people dismiss John Brown as a lunatic or homicidal maniac. They may be influenced by John Steuart Curry's mural in Topeka. It portrays him as a wild-eyed, fiery, larger-than-life madman. And before I read much about John Brown or the turbulent time he lived in, I agreed.

But after I read several biographies, I changed my mind. He was a zealot. He (or the men he led) did kill five men — a criminal act. He *was* a single-minded, fanatical abolitionist. But he cared deeply about the enslaved blacks.

Ever since as a child he saw a black boy severely beaten by a slaveowner, he vowed to free all slaves. It became an obsession. So, when he came to Kansas during the turbulent 1850's, he joined the violence characteristic of the place and time. Both sides in the conflict were violent and bloody. He was no better and no worse than other factional leaders of his day.

John Brown was a deeply religious man, and, like many others, he found biblical support for the abolitionist cause. People like John Greenleaf Whittier and Henry David Thoreau believed Brown was doing the right thing in campaigning for Kansas to become a free-soil state. The popular song "John Brown's Body," known even today by almost everybody, gives powerful evidence that he was revered as much as he was reviled — particularly after he became a synonym for abolition after 1859.

When Brown went to Harper's Ferry, Virginia, with only a handful of men to free the slaves on a national scale, he believed that the blacks merely needed weapons and an opportunity to revolt. He thought the blacks would fight for freedom on their own, inspired by an idealist like himself. He simply miscalculated. He was captured by Robert E. Lee, tried, condemned, and hanged in 1859.

Ultimately, of course, his action was a key event leading to the national calamity of 1861-1865, the Civil War.

JOHN BROWN

The zeal of the Lord,
　　The zeal of the Lord of Hosts was upon him.
One thing did he desire,
　　One thing only:
He vowed to free all slaves.
　　As a child he saw a black boy beaten
　　And he vowed to free all slaves.
He came to Kansas to keep her soil free.
　　He came with guns to fight for freedom.
　　He came to Osawatomie.
He came with a prophet's dream.
　　He came with piercing blue eyes
　　And an iron will.
He was a Moses among men.
　　He set out with his sons to help Lawrence,
　　But the city was already in flames.
He returned to Pottawatomie with a posse
　　And they killed five men.
　　Five pro-slavery men.
He then left Kansas with a grand plan
　　To free all slaves.
　　He helped eleven flee to Canada.
Soon he went to Harper's Ferry
　　With twenty-one men
　　To free all slaves.
Was he mad? Was he a saint?
　　The questions are irrelevant.
His head was in the clouds
　　While his feet trod on the earth.
　　The zeal of the Lord of Hosts consumed him.

NICODEMUS

Nicodemus was an all black colony established in Graham County in 1877. W.R. Hill, founder of nearby Hill City, conceived the idea of creating a town for the recently freed slaves and engaged the help of W.H. Smith, a black, to fulfill the plan. They established the Nicodemus Town Company and charged five dollars for each settler to join the settlement. It was American entrepreneurship at work, as they attempted to create a boom town in a sparsely populated part of the state. They located on the south fork of the Solomon River.

The blacks joined the effort — Z.T. Fletcher, Simon P. Roundtree, Edward P. McCabe, Daniel Hickman — and on September 17, 1877, three hundred black settlers arrived. In the spring of 1879 two hundred more appeared, then several smaller groups, until by 1880 the population was about five hundred people. But the land was forbidding. The first settlers lived in dugouts and arrived too late in the season to get crops in. They had no proper equipment, and money was scarce. Food supplies were almost non-existent. Not surprisingly, many people left.

The survivors had high hopes for a railroad line coming through or near the town. A railroad would assure the town's success. They dickered with the Missouri Pacific Railroad first, then with the Santa Fe and the Central Branch of the Union Pacific. Early signs were encouraging, but each road in turn chose another route. And the town, like most other by-passed settlements, dwindled. By the mid-twentieth century the town still exists, but it numbers only a few families.

On August first each year, however, former residents and descendants of former residents return to Nicodemus for an annual reunion and festival of memories. It's a grand homecoming.

NICODEMUS

Black town, boom town,
Promised land for freedmen
Armed with dreams and courage
On the Great High Plains.

Black town, boom town,
Struggled for a foothold,
Fought the drouth and locusts
In an alien land.

Black town, boom town,
Flourished like a spring shoot,
Vying for a railroad
Till the Roads said No.

Boom town, black town,
Scattered to new Edens,
Left their Kansas haven
As the bubble burst.

Boom town, black town,
Shriveled like a raisin,
Peopled by a remnant
Who would not say die.

Black town, boom town,
Symbol of a proud folk,
Celebrate their mem'ries
Every August first.

JOHN NOBLE

John Noble was born in Wichita in 1874. He decided at age fifteen to be a painter. His family was wealthy and wanted John to choose a money-making career, but he was firm. He would be a painter. His first commission was for the Carey House Bar. The owners wanted the painting of a nude woman over the bar, and John painted "Cleopatra at the Bath" for them (Carrie Nation shortly thereafter pretty well demolished it with her hatchet).

John had to get away, he felt, if he were to become the painter he dreamed about. So he went to Paris where he joined a colony of artists living in an old remodeled barn called the *Ruche*. Here he met leading artists like Matisse and Picasso and developed his unique style. He became an internationally recognized artist although he is not popularly known.

He loved the sea and people of the sea, and painted many seascapes. Some of his best known paintings from Europe are *Low Tide, Pont Croix, Launching the Boat, Blue Moonlight, Toilers of the Sea, Harbor by Moonlight, The Boat Horses, Breton Fishermen*, and *Baiting the Lines*. Later he moved to Provincetown, Massachusetts, where he continued to paint scenes related to the sea: *Sardine Fishermen, Mending the Nets, The Ice Cutters*, and *Provincetown Winter*. He tended to paint natural scenes in which people appear only incidentally, for the generations pass away but the earth abideth forever. The Wichita Center for the Arts owns several of his works. He died in 1934.

Like Vincent Van Gogh or D.H. Lawrence, John drove restlessly for perfection in art — and never found it. He married, had a loving wife and many friends, but he drove moodily and restlessly towards an elusive ideal in art. He was a turbulent, driven man.

JOHN NOBLE

He painted from his heart.
Wichita Bill, they called him
As he shared *la Roche*
With artists like himself in Paris.
He played the part with gusto, horse
And Stetson, snakeskin vest
And hair like Cody's.
But the sea and people of the sea
Were his subjects — not the West.
He painted them in aching loneliness,
Driven by a demon to find beauty
And to capture truth.
He tried to paint his way to peace
But never found his way.
He sought a great white buffalo
And thought it represented death.
Or God. Or work. Or self. Or love.
He drowned himself in spirits —
Whiskey Bill — as clouds of night
Oppressed his soul.
He loved the North Star —
Steady beacon in a shadowy world.
His *Toilers of the Sea*, *Breton Fishing Village*,
And *Sardine Fishermen* are haunting scenes
Of simple lives and grueling days.
He reached for more forever,
Never finding harbor, overcome too often
By a black despair.
But the beauty remains.

WINDMILLS

Silhouettes stand clear
Against a western sky
With orange sun sliced neatly
To the traveler's view
By windmills,
Some complete and turning high above the plain,
Some without a blade or two,
And still —
Or limping,
Pounding with ill-meshing gears.
Some huddled heaps of twisted steel
Speak silently
Of crippling storms and vanished past,
Of pioneers who fought the elements —
And lost.
They stayed to see the prairie tamed,
Though broken like their mills
And cast aside.
The rest responded to the soil
Like windmills to the wind
And faced their fate
With wills of steel,
Though gaunt
And weathered from incessant toil.

AMELIA EARHART

Amelia Earhart (AE) became America's darling in 1928 when she was the first woman to fly the Atlantic. She was a passenger on *The Friendship*, a single engine Fokker plane, the first woman to do it.

She was born in Atchison, Kansas, on July 24, 1897, at her grandfather's house. During the next few years she and her sister Muriel spent a great deal of time in Atchison at her grandfather's home on Quality Hill, now an AE museum.

She early was a tomboy and dared to do about anything that seemed possible. She wasn't about to let boys have all the fun and excitement. Gradually, as a result of family pressures, she became more and more independent and alone. Under her picture in the high school annual is the legend, "The girl in brown who walks alone."

She learned to fly in California with Neta Snook and by 1920 was a licensed pilot. On her twenty-fourth birthday she bought her first plane, a Kinner Canary. From then on she was an inveterate flyer, flying all points in the country. Conditions were incredibly primitive: there were no paved runways, planes were experimental and unreliable, accidents were common (Amelia herself crashed her planes several times) and airport facilities were crude.

After the 1928 flight across the Atlantic, the event which brought her international fame, she was a public figure. In 1932 she flew solo across the Atlantic to remove the stigma of her passenger status in 1928. In 1934 she flew solo from Hawaii to California, then in 1935 solo from Los Angeles to Mexico City. In 1937 she flew east to west on an abortive round the world trip that ended in Hawaii, then reversed directions and flew eastward around the world at the equator until she disappeared at sea just east of New Guinea in the Pacific Ocean.

Rescuers searched intensely for her, but no sign of her ill-fated plane was ever found. She missed tiny Howland Island and presumably ran out of fuel and plunged to the ocean floor.

AMELIA EARHART

Firmly assertive,
Untamed, unrestrained,
A tomgirl in Atchison.

"The girl in brown
Who walks alone,"
They said,
A solitary soul.

She fell in love with flying
And flew "for the fun of it."
She sported leather clothes, those days,
And bobbed her hair.

In 'twenty-eight
She crossed to Wales
(With comb and toothbrush)
In a trimotor Fokker.
In 'thirty-two she soloed
To Ireland in a single engine Lockheed.

She pioneered on unpaved fields
With experimental aircraft,
A flying vagabond across the land.

But courage was her watchword
And self-confidence her style.
She was warm and feminine
But knew she could do
As well as Wiley Post or
Lucky Lindy — and did.

Her last flight in 'thirty-seven
Ended in disaster near Howland Isle,
A dot in the Pacific,
Shrouded in mystery.

Yet her indomitable spirit
Lives and speaks across the years.

WILLIAM ALLEN WHITE

Words were his life.
Good words. Hard words. Firm words. The right words.
Will loved people,
And he set out by words to create a better world.
He started with Emporia and Kansas
And he never got over his love affair with them,
Even when he was a world figure.
He wanted no office; he would be hostage to no one.
He wrote about ordinary people with grace and sensitivity.
He loved to talk and listen to good talk more than anything else.
He wrote stories and verse, but his editorials and obituaries
    and personals were the stuff of his life.
He made enemies, but he also made a host of friends.
He took sides. He changed gradually over the years as he grew,
    early a conservative, late a liberal.
He admired Lincoln; he loved Teddy Roosevelt.
He gave jobs to dozens of young writers, launching them
    on careers.
His red fountain pen was eloquent.
The Sage of Emporia will long be honored for his
    homespun wisdom expressed as it was in
    clear, simple words.

DWIGHT DAVID EISENHOWER

Raised in Abilene,
The third of six sons, he
Learned to face his challengers
Face to face.
At twelve he chose to die
Rather than lose a leg
To blood poisoning —
But lived.
At twenty he won his way
To West Point and at
Twenty-six to Mamie's heart.

At fifty-one he had
His first star, and by
Fifty-three was Supreme
Commander of the Allied Force.
At sixty-two he took the
Oath of Office to defend
The Constitution as the thirty-fourth
President.

He came from the heart of America.
He fought with skill
But peace was ever his goal.
He avoided confrontation and was,
Withal, another Pericles,
A child of destiny.

Duty was his watchword —
He never shrank from it.
He was a great man
With a simple heart
And a simple faith
In his fellows
And in God.

POST ROCK

Post rock fences
With their barbed wire strands
Watch with steady purpose
Over treeless lands.

Limestone quarry —
Markings line each edge,
Hallmarks of the forceful
Feathers, drill, and wedge.

Brown streaked sentries
Wearing ripe grain hue
Stand at rapt attention
As in full review.

Soft when quarried,
Turning hard when dried,
The posts like soldiers
Stand in serried pride.

Old time settlers
Carved a life from stone,
Raised their crops and cattle —
Each man fenced his own.

Post rock fences
Stand erect today,
A hundred years of service
Just like yesterday.

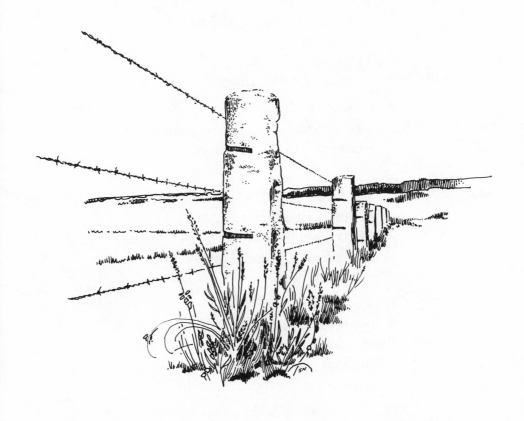

KARL MENNINGER

He probed the depths of the mind.
He dug and dug
Until he found companion lodes
Of hate and love,
Of Thanatos and Eros,
At the heart of humankind.

A psychoanalyst was, he said,
A diplomat, detective, scientist, and priest,
Magician, therapist, and doctor,
All in one.

He sought the secrets of the inner life
And found a vital balance
At the core of healthy minds
Where faith and love and hope reside —
The greatest, hope!

His ego was enough for two,
A driving force that jostled
Friends and foes alike,
As Dr. Karl probed on and on
For answers to the mysteries of life.

He thought analysis the one right way
To ferret out unconscious wounds
And deeply hidden guilt and sin
And built an empire on that base.

GORDON PARKS

He saw through the lens with his heart.
His *American Gothic*
Speaks of poverty and pain and loss
And pride and fortitude and courage.
His Harlem shots of garbage cans,
Of crowded beds and fallen plaster,
Infested rooms and filthy alleys
Peopled plentifully with ragged urchins,
Desperate men with vacant eyes,
Proud women holding things together
With a thin, fine thread of hope —
He caught it all in the black and whites
That he shared through *Life*.

Born in Fort Scott, he began there
To bear the burden of being black
But he fought the odds and
Became a piano player,
Playing the blacks and whites,

Became a composer and wrote "No Love"
Became a filmmaker and made *The Learning Tree*
Became a poet and novelist
Became a photographer and filmed the world,
Telling the story of blacks and whites.

KANSAS

The years 1855 through 1860 saw much travail in Kansas Territory when the subject of statehood was proposed because the South wanted to admit her as a slave state and Free-soilers and Abolitionists did not. Missouri, a border slave state, sent citizens to vote and agitate for slavery in the territory. Free-slavers across the country became involved and sent money and settlers to assure that the proposed state would be free of slavery. The struggle was bitter and bloody, more so than can be summarized in a few words.

John Brown in 1856 assembled a small group and one night near Pottawatomie murdered five pro-slavers in cold blood. Two years later, almost to the date, Charles Hamilton, a Georgian come to Kansas, captured nine Free-Soilers with his company of men. He took them to a gulch on the Marais des Cygnes river, lined them up and summarily shot them. Five died on the spot, four were wounded and, by playing dead, escaped to tell the story. Jayhawks, one story goes, worried their prey as a cat torments a mouse, making themselves a threat to the peace of all border pro-slavers. Redlegs, led by James Lane and Charles Jennison, were part of a brutal fast-moving squadron of Free-soilers who wore red morocco leggings. The Missourians responded in kind as Border Ruffians, and so the struggle raged back and forth.

Perhaps the most cowardly and outrageous event occurred after Kansas became a state, when, half way through the Civil War, William Quantrill raided Lawrence, a Free-soil center. He surprised the city at daybreak on August 20, 1863, with a party of 294 men and set out to kill every male and to burn every house. Within a few hours, 183 men and boys lay dead, and most of the houses lay in ruin.

It is these kinds of outrage on both sides that marked the years 1855-1861 as a prelude to admission of Kansas into the Union as the thirty-fourth state under President James Buchanan.

AD ASTRA PER ASPERA

They called her "bleeding Kansas" in those days
As she reached for the stars in hardy ways,
Beset by factions in the Great Debate.
Free-soilers and Pro-slavers could not wait —
They lined up partisans to plead their cause
Then turned to bullets rather than to laws.
Brown's bloody Pottawatomie affair
Was matched when Hamilton refused to spare
His captives. Jayhawks (later Redlegs) crossed
The river on forays. Nothing lost,
Missouri sent her Quantrills, soon and late,
And bloodbaths multiplied at frightful rate.
But Kansas came a state in sixty-one,
A six-year fight at length by Free-soil won,
And placed her star with thirty-three on a field
Of blue — her place with difficulty sealed.

COLOPHON

Raymond S. Nelson, Ph.D. taught English for thirty-three years at two institutions, Morningside College in Sioux City, Iowa, and Friends University in Wichita, Kansas. He has published three books of poetry, *Not by Bread Alone* (1982), *Reflections on Life: Birth to Death* (1987), and *Tracings* (1989).

The artist, R. Stanley Nelson, is Dr. Nelson's son. He is a Museum Specialist at the Smithsonian Museum of American History, Washington, D.C. His specialty is type-casting, an important dimension to the history of printing.

The type face is Janson, printed on 60# Natural Nekoosa Opaque Offset paper.